# PATENT AN ASSET TO BUSINESS

A Practical Guide for
Entrepreneurs and Inventors

Copyright © 2020 DHANANJAY MODGALYA

All rights reserved

No part of this book may be reproduced, or stored in a retrieval system, or transmitted in any form or by any means, electronic, mechanical, photocopying, recording, or otherwise, without express written permission of the publisher.

Dedicated to my Parents

# Table of Content

## Chapter 1 - Introduction to Intellectual Property . 7
What is Intellectual Property ..............................7
Property......................................................8
Patent .......................................................10
Trademark ...................................................10
Copyright....................................................12
Industrial Design............................................13
Geographical Indication......................................14
Semiconductor Circuit Layout.................................15
Plant Varieties..............................................16
Brief History of Intellectual Property.......................16

## Chapter 2 - Indian Patent System .........................19
History of Indian Patent Law.................................19
What is Patentable...........................................22
Non-patentable Inventions....................................24
Who can File a Patent .......................................27
How to File a Patent ........................................28
Priority Date................................................29
How to Ascertain Patentability ..............................30
What is not Anticipation ....................................31
Patent Process ..............................................34
.............................................................35

## Chapter 3 - Patent Analytics for Business................37
Prior Art Search ............................................37
Art of Searching.............................................38
Where to Search..............................................39
Freedom to Operate...........................................40
Invalidation Search..........................................40

Landscape Search ..................................................40

## Chapter 4 - Patent Specification ..........................42
Description ............................................................42
Drawings................................................................43
Claims ....................................................................43
Abstract .................................................................44

## Chapter 5 - Patent Procedures ............................46
Filing .....................................................................46
Publication............................................................46
Secrecy Direction .................................................47
Foreign Filing License .........................................48
Amendments.........................................................48
Examination .........................................................49
Grant......................................................................52
Appeal ...................................................................54
Renewal.................................................................54

## Chapter 6 - Type of Patent Application..............58
Ordinary Application ..........................................58
Convention Application ......................................59
PCT application ...................................................61
Divisional application ..........................................62
Patent of Addition................................................63

## Chapter 7 - Opposition..........................................66
Type of Opposition ..............................................66
Grounds of Opposition........................................66
Who can File an Opposition ...............................70
Procedure of Opposition .....................................70

## Chapter 8 - Patent Infringement..........................74
Filing Suits in Courts...........................................74
Defenses to Infringements...................................76
Fair Use.................................................................78

Revocation .............................................................79
Injunction .............................................................83
Groundless Threats ............................................83
Settlements ..........................................................84

**Chapter 9 - Rights of Patentee..............................87**
Right to Exploit Patent.......................................87
Right to License ..................................................87
Right to Assign ....................................................88
Right to Mortgage...............................................88
Right to Lease......................................................88
Right to Surrender..............................................89
Right against Infringement...............................89
Enforcement of Patent........................................89

**Chapter 10 - Commercialization of Patent...........91**
Use ........................................................................91
License .................................................................91
Technology Transfer ..........................................92
Compulsory Licensing........................................92

**Chapter 11 - PCT Application...............................95**
PCT International Application..........................95
International Publication ..................................96
International Search...........................................96
International Preliminary Examination ..........96
National Phase Applications .............................96

**Chapter 12 - Startups and IP.................................99**
Definition of Startup...........................................99
Benefits to Startup ............................................100
Expedited Examination ....................................100

# Preface

Intellectual property has been the center stage of development and all the companies want to protect their creation, which is being difficult by the non-availability of information. There are several ways to commercialize the invention, which has been discussed for the benefit of all.

There are special provisions for the startup in terms of benefit over IP protection, which must be known to all entrepreneurs.

A Patent is an asset to the business and it must be exploited, protected, and enforced for the profit of the business.

This book will help you understand the process of patent and what to do and what not to do. A special focus has been provided for prior art searches and what innovators can utilize for better invention.

I thank all my teachers and family for their support.

# Chapter 1 - Introduction to Intellectual Property

## What is Intellectual Property

Intellectual property generally refers to the creation of the mind. There is no formal definition of intellectual property as a creation of the mind has many facets. Intellectual property can be anything that comes out of the creativity and intelligence of a human mind. Intellectual property is a buzzword in the modern era. Everybody is encountering the word "Intellectual Property" in one form or another in every walk of life.

Human creativity has a vast canvas and the creation of a human mind does not belong to one set of creations. Intellectual property rights are ever-growing and accordingly, new kinds of intellectual property are included with time.

There are several types of intellectual property categorized by different laws and the World Intellectual Property Organization (WIPO). Commonly known IPs are patent, copyright, trademark, industrial design, geographical indication, plant varieties, and semiconductor integrated circuit layout.

when a person creates something he wants to commercialize the output which he is right to do as the owner or the creator and his right must be recognized over his creation. Otherwise, there will be no reason for any person to delve into the creation and that will hinder the progress of society, which depends on the creation of new and original things.

If intellectual property is not protected the owner will keep creation as secret and will not divulge the information to the public which in turn hamper the progress of society, as the effort of society as a whole will go into the futile process of re-inventing the wheel.

When a person invents a new product or process and does not disclose the same to the world, not all inventors or creators are businessmen. Disclosure without protection will lead to loss of his labor, creativity, and effort. Unless he commercializes on his own invention will be kept secret. Then again another person facing the same problem has to reinvent the wheel and in this way, the invention of the wheel will continue till it comes to the public domain, and then only another person can try to work on further inventions. A lack of information which must be dealt with else reinventing the wheel continues.

Intellectual property must be protected so that the creator or inventor will provide disclosure to the public for the furtherance of the progress of society and ease in commercial utilization of the invention.

## Property

Property is mainly categorized as tangible property

and intangible property. Tangible or corporeal property is related to material things, which can be seen and measured, while the intangible property is those properties that cannot be seen.

In general reference to a property is taken as corporeal property which can be understood by visual and other sensory phenomena and the rights defined in a corporeal property are easier to understand in terms of possession and ownership because a tangible property has to be in the possession of one person or a group of people, like land, vehicle, money, and house, etc.

Intangible property refers to the property which cannot be seen or touched. It is the creation of the mind and the mind only can perceive it. It is the property that can be passed to another person and still retained. Just like knowledge, if you give knowledge to somebody you still have it. Having such characteristics, the intangible property has to be treated in a separate way.

This is the reason why an intellectual property has been defined separately, to acknowledge the right of the creator. The creation of the human mind should be the property of the owner so he has right over his creation even if the possession goes into another's hand.

The information and knowledge can be freely traded, as the sovereign will give protection against any potential infringement in return for public disclosure.

Intellectual property is a tangible property that deals with the fruit of labor by using knowledge, creativity, and intellect.

Intellectual property is an exclusive right which also grants Monopoly over the creation.

## Patent

A patent is an exclusive right granted by the sovereign to an inventor for a limited period of time in exchange for the disclosure of the invention.

Being an exclusive right, the owner has not only the right to use but also the right to exclude others. The moment an invention is created, it can be used subject to the rights of other persons. Though the whole point of the grant of an exclusive right is to exclude others from utilizing the invention without the permission of the owner. Also, if somebody will infringe upon his right by way of exploiting an invention in any way without the approval of the owner then the owner has the right to stop him and claim damages.

The patent right has quid pro quo inbuilt in the statute. In exchange for the patent right, the patent owner makes technical information about the invention publicly available in the published patent document, the reason behind the disclosure is that the community as a whole will try to invent something new over it and somebody will not put his own time, effort and money to invent the same invention for the sake of faster technical progress of the world.

## Trademark

A mark, which distinguishes goods or services of one person from another is a Trademark. A mark may be in the form of a device, brand, heading, label, name, signature, word, letter, shape of packaging or combination of colors, or any combination thereof.

In India, the trademark must be capable of being represented graphically, it must be capable of distinguishing the goods or services of one person from those of another for getting registration under the Indian law. Trademarks must be used or proposed to be used in relation to goods or services. The use must be for the purpose of indicating a connection in the course of trade between the goods or services and some persons having the right as the proprietor to use the mark.

The right to proprietorship of a trademark may be acquired by registration under the Trademark Act or by use in relation to goods or services.

Trademark is the brand identity in any form which can be designated to particular goods or services of the proprietor and it has the capability of distinguishing the goods or services of another person.

Trademarks can be in any form and even smell marks are recognized around the world, but in India, smell mark has not been registered because smell marks cannot be graphically represented yet. The smell of fresh-cut grass for tennis balls has been registered as a trademark in Europe.

Three essential components of the trademark are a proprietor, mark, and goods or services. The basic feature of a trademark is a user will associate a mark on the goods or services to a particular proprietor. In turn, the user will associate the quality of the product as being originated from the proprietor and the goodwill associated with him.

Trademark is one of the most important parts of any business and this intellectual property is very much in use for a long time and there have been more disputes over brand alone than any other kind of intellectual property. The basic doctrine of trademark revolves around the likelihood of confusion in the mind of a user.

As a business one must be aware of trademarks as once a brand will infringe the right of prior users of such brand identity, the whole business may collapse. As changing brand identity will bring loss of goodwill acquired.

## Copyright

Copyright means the exclusive right to do or authorize others to do certain acts in relation to original literary, dramatic, musical, and artistic works, cinematograph film, and sound recording.

Copyright is an exclusive right which prevents others from taking benefit of the fruit of labor and skill of another person.

The rightful owner of the copyright in any creation has the right to exclude others from utilizing it or adapting it and even translating it in any form.

In India for published literary, dramatic, musical, and artistic work protection is for 60 years from the death of the author. In the case of photographs, it is 60 years from the beginning of the calendar year following the publication. For cinematographic films and sound recording, copyright will subsist until 60 years from the publication of work.

Unlike the patent and trademark, copyright protection is from the date of creation while in patent and Trademark protection is given from the date of filing application with the concerned authority.

## Industrial Design

Design means only the features or a configuration of ornament or composition of lines or colors applied to any article whether in two-dimensional and three-dimensional or in both forms by an industrial process or means, which in the finished article appeal to and are solely by the eye, but does not include any mode or principle of construction or anything which is in substance.

A design must be novel or original and has not been disclosed to the public anywhere in India or any other country by publication in any form or by use or in any other way prior to the filing date or is not significantly distinguishable from known designs or combination of known designs for comprises of or contains a scandalous obsession matter.

When a design is registered the registered proprietor of the design shall have copyright in the design for 10 years from the date of registration and which may be extended for the second period of five years from the expiration of the original period of 10 years.

The most important factor of an industrial design is that it must be appealing to the eye and also have a functional characteristic.

The copyright subsists in aesthetics only but industrial design functionality is also important. Otherwise, the aesthetics of the design should be copyrighted only.

## Geographical Indication

Geographical indication in relation to goods means an indication which identifies such goods as agriculture, agricultural goods, natural goods or manufactured goods as originating or manufactured in the territory of a country or region or locality. Where given quality, reputation or another characteristic of such goods is essentially attributable to its geographical origin and in a case where such goods are manufactured goods, one of the activities of either the production of processing on the preparation of the goods takes place in such region or locality.

Any association of persons or producers or any organization or authority representing the interest of the producers, in the territory, of the concerned goods who are desirous of registering a geographical indication in relation to such good shall apply to the registrar.

One of the most prominent features which must be described as a particular or a specific quality, reputation or other characteristics, which are attributable exclusive or essentially to the geographical environment with its inherent natural and human factors and the production or processing for preparation that takes place in region or locality.

## Semiconductor Circuit Layout

Semiconductor Integrated circuit layout design has been defined as a layout of transistors and other circuitry elements and indicates live lead wire connecting such elements and expressed in any manner in a semiconductor Integrated circuit.

Integrated Circuit layout must be original and has not been commercially exploited anywhere in India or in a convention country. Also, it should be inherently distinctive and which is inherently capable of being distinguishable from any other registered layout design.

## Plant Varieties

A new variety of plants can be registered under the law only if it satisfies the requirement of novelty, distinctiveness, uniformity, and stability, also it has not been commercially used before the date of application.

## Brief History of Intellectual Property

The term intellectual property refers to a cluster of legal rights that regulate the use of different sorts of ideas and the creation of minds is the intangible property which originates from an idea to an expression and the expression is usable.

The history of intellectual property can be traced back to ancient Greece, wherein the $7^{th}$ century BC monopolies were granted for the new recipes. In the Roman empire monopoly granted for the creation of silk and in 1432 the Senate of Venice enacted the statute for providing the exclusive right to the invention of the machine and process.

In 1474 first Ordinance in patent came into existence in Venice. Statute of Anne, 1710 on copyright was enacted in England which is one of the earliest statutes on copyright.

The Statute of Monopolies was an Act of the Parliament of England for invention, which is one of the earliest statutes on the patent.

In the US the copyright act of 1790 enacted and it granted the exclusive right for a limited period of time in literary and artistic creations.

On the global scale the Paris Convention 1883 and Berne Convention 1886, which was subsequently merged in 1893 and adopted the term intellectual property. Further in 1960, United International bureaucrats for the protection of intellectual property was located in Geneva and in 1967 World Intellectual Property Organization (WIPO) was established by a treaty which is a leading agency of United Nation and take care of intellectual property Regime all over the world.

The major globalization event was the creation of Trade-Related aspects of Intellectual Property Rights (TRIPS) on January 1, 1995. The main objective of the TRIPs is bring uniformity in patent law around the world, where some deviations has been allowed based on public policy and need of specific country.

# Chapter 2 - Indian Patent System

## History of Indian Patent Law

Indian patent law came into force when India became a colony of the British Empire in 1856 when protection of invention was based on British patent law of 1852. The Act was modified in 1859 and certain exclusive privileges were granted to inventors for making, selling, and using inventions in India and authorizing others to do so for 14 years.

The first Patent and design Protection Act was enacted in 1872. The Indian patents and design Act was enacted in 1911 which was amended in 1950 and compulsory licensing and working of the invention along with revocation was added.

The Indian Patent Bill 1953 was introduced in Lok Sabha but it could not be passed. For the working of the patent system in India under the chairmanship of N. Rajagopala Ayyangar, a committee was established for the creation of the Patent Act, which submitted its report in 1959 and in 1965 the patent bill was introduced but again lapsed do to the dissolution of Lok Sabha.

Then in 1970, the patent bill was again introduced in Parliament and it was enacted as the Indian Patents Act 1970 which remained in force till December 1994 and two ordinances were introduced one in 1994 and another in 1999 which was primarily due to the association of TRIPS and to establish the conformity with the TRIPS. The Indian patent law has to be amended and the ordinance was introduced to include product patent and the exclusive marketing rights were provided till 31st December 2004 for several entities as product patent was not available in India before January 2005.

The Patents (Amendment) Act, 2002 included the new Patent Rules, 2003 replacing the Patent Rules of 1972 and there was a third amendment by patent amendment Ordinance in 2004 which was replaced by patent (Amendment) Act 2005.

The Patent rules have been amended several times and in the last few years. There were several amendments to the promotion of patents in India and fees have been changed several times.

In the Patent (Amendment) Rules, 2016 startup was defined and several benefits for a startup in respect of fees were also included. In the Patent (Second Amendment) Rules, 2020 small entities registered with MSME can also avail fee reduction at par with startups.

The patent office has been established in all four metro cities Kolkata, Delhi, Mumbai, and Chennai, wherein Kolkata being the head office

The office of controller general of patents, designs, and trademarks is located in Mumbai.

Mumbai patent office has territorial jurisdiction over Maharashtra, Gujarat, Madhya Pradesh, Goa and Chhattisgarh and union territories of Daman and Diu and Dadra and Nagar Haveli.

Chennai patent office has the territorial jurisdiction over Andhra Pradesh, Karnataka, Kerala, Tamilnadu, and the union territories of Pondicherry Lakshadweep and Telangana.

New Delhi patent office has the territorial jurisdiction over Haryana, Himachal Pradesh, Jammu and Kashmir, Punjab, Rajasthan, Uttar Pradesh, Uttaranchal, Delhi, and the union territory of Chandigarh.

Kolkata patent office has jurisdiction over the rest of India

## What is Patentable

Any new invention is patentable under Indian patent law, there are exceptions in the subject matter of the patentable invention.

The primary criterion for a new invention is that it should be novel and not anticipated anywhere by any Publication or use, it has inventiveness and it should be capable of industrial application.

Novelty could be checked through a thorough prior art search of patent and literature available throughout the world.

Inventive step or non-obviousness can be check through the structured approach commended in Windsurfing International Inc. v. Tabur Marine (Great Britain) Ltd. and

1. Identify the notional "person skilled in the art" and identify the relevant common general knowledge of that person;
2. Identify the inventive concept of the claim of alleged invention or if that cannot readily be done, construe the claim;
3. Identify if any differences exist between the matter forming part of the state of the art and the inventive concept of the claim or the claim as construed;

4. Understand without using any knowledge of the alleged invention as claimed, do those differences constitute steps which would have been obvious to the person skilled in the art, or do they require any degree of invention.

The person skilled in the art should be construed as a person having ordinary intellect and having knowledge of prior art related to the field. He need not be an expert with high intellect.

The Indian Patent Act, 1970 defines invention and inventive steps under section 2 as:

*"new invention" means any invention or technology which has not been anticipated by publication in any document or used in the country or elsewhere in the world before the date of filing of a patent application with complete specification, i.e., the subject matter has not fallen in the public domain or that it does not form part of the state of the art.*

*"invention" means a new product or process involving an inventive step and capable of industrial application.*

*"inventive step" means a feature of an invention that involves technical advance as compared to the existing knowledge or having economic significance*

*or both and that makes the invention not obvious to a person skilled in the art.*

## Non-patentable Inventions

No patent shall be granted in respect of an invention relating to atomic energy. Further, the followings are not patentable under Section 3 of the Indian Patents Act, 1970

(a) an invention which is frivolous or which claims anything obviously contrary to well established natural laws;

(b) an invention the primary or intended use or commercial exploitation of which could be contrary to public order or morality or which causes serious prejudice to human, animal or plant life or health or to the environment;

(c) the mere discovery of a scientific principle or the formulation of an abstract theory or discovery of any living thing or non-living substance occurring in nature;

(d) the mere discovery of a new form of a known substance which does not result in the enhancement of the known efficacy of that substance or the mere discovery of any new property or new use for a known substance or of the mere use of a known process, machine or apparatus unless such known process results in a new product or employs at least one new reactant.

Explanation.—For the purposes of this clause, salts,

esters, ethers, polymorphs, metabolites, pure form, particle size, isomers, mixtures of isomers, complexes, combinations, and other derivatives of known substance shall be considered to be the same substance, unless they differ significantly in properties with regard to efficacy;

(e) a substance obtained by a mere admixture resulting only in the aggregation of the properties of the components thereof or a process for producing such substance;

(f) the mere arrangement or re-arrangement or duplication of known devices each functioning independently of one another in a known way;

(h) a method of agriculture or horticulture;

(i) any process for the medicinal, surgical, curative, prophylactic diagnostic, therapeutic, or other treatment of human beings or any process for a similar treatment of animals to render them free of disease or to increase their economic value or that of their products.

(j) plants and animals in whole or any part thereof other than micro- organisms but including seeds, varieties, and species and essentially biological processes for production or propagation of plants and animals;

(k) a mathematical or business method or a computer programme per se or algorithms;

(l) a literary, dramatic, musical or artistic work or any other aesthetic creation whatsoever including cinematographic works and television productions;

(m) a mere scheme or rule or method of performing mental act or method of playing game;

(n) a presentation of information;

(o) topography of integrated circuits;

(p) an invention which in effect, is traditional knowledge or which is an aggregation or duplication of known properties of a traditionally known component or components.

The Computer program per se is not patentable, while a computer program with a novel hardware combination can be patentable.

Further, in a recent judgment in the case *Ferid Allani vs Union Of India & Ors* dated 12 December 2019 the Delhi High Court states:
*"In todays digital world, when most inventions are based on computer programs, it would be retrograde to argue that all such inventions would not be patentable. Innovation in the field of artificial intelligence, blockchain technologies and other digital products would be based on computer programs, however the same would not become non*

*patentable inventions – simply for that reason. It is rare to see a product which is not based on a computer program. Whether they are cars and other automobiles, microwave ovens, washing machines, refrigerators, they all have some sort of computer programs in-built in them. Thus, the effect that such programs produce including in digital and electronic products is crucial in determining the test of patentability."*

## Who can File a Patent

An application for a patent for an invention may be made by any of the following persons, as per Section 6 of the Indian Patents Act, that is to say,—

(a) by any person claiming to be the true and first inventor of the invention;

(b) by any person being the assignee of the person claiming to be the true and first inventor in respect of the right to make such an application;

(c) by the legal representative of any deceased person who immediately before his death was entitled to make such an application.

The application can be made by any person alone or jointly.

Where the application is made by virtue of an assignment of the right to apply for a patent for the invention, proof of right in terms of assignment deed or any other contract needs to be provided to the Patent Office.

If any person is, by reason of minority, lunacy or other disability, incapable of making any statement or doing anything required or permitted by or under this Act, the lawful guardian, committee or manager (if any) of the person subject to the disability, or if there be none, any person appointed by any court possessing jurisdiction in respect of his property, may make such statement or a statement as nearly corresponding thereto as circumstances permit, and do such thing in the name and on behalf of the person subject to the disability.

## How to File a Patent

Every application for a patent shall be for one invention only.

Every such application shall be accompanied by a provisional or a complete specification.

Every application under this section shall state that the applicant is in possession of the invention and shall name the person claiming to be the true and first inventor. Where the person so claiming is not the applicant or one of the applicants, the application shall contain a declaration that the applicant believes the person so named to be the true and first inventor.

The Applicant can file patent applications by themselves or through a registered patent agent only.

Patent Application has to be filed in an online or offline format and the patent office should be selected as per the jurisdiction of the patent office.

## Priority Date

The priority date is the most important aspect of a patent application as all rights and anticipations are from the priority date. The applicant must ensure an early priority date to secure a patent.

Ideally, the priority date is the date of the first filing of the application and whatever is disclosed in the application shall have such a priority date.

There shall be a priority date for each claim of a complete specification. Where a complete specification is filed in pursuance of a single application accompanied by a provisional specification and the claim is fairly based on the matter disclosed in the specification the priority date of that claim shall be the date of the filing of the relevant specification.

Where the complete specification is filed or proceeded with in pursuance of two or more applications accompanied by such specifications and the claim is fairly based on the matter disclosed in one of those specifications, the priority date of that claim shall be the date of the filing of the application accompanied by that specification.

Where a complete specification based on a previously filed application in India has been filed within twelve months from the date of that application and the claim is fairly based on the matter disclosed in the previously filed application, the priority date of that claim shall be the date of the previously filed application in which the matter was first disclosed.

Where the complete specification has been filed in pursuance of a further application made as divisional application and the claim is fairly based on the matter disclosed in any of the earlier specifications, provisional or complete, as the case may be, the priority date of that claim shall be the date of the filing of that specification in which the matter was first disclosed.

The reference to the date of the filing of the application or of the complete specification shall, in cases where there has been a post-dating or antedating, be a reference to the date as so post-dated or ante-dated.

An application can be post-dated if required by the applicant.

## How to Ascertain Patentability

To ascertain an invention is patentable, the first criteria have to be looked at as the novelty of the invention. The invention must be novel that means a new invention that has not been disclosed in any publication anywhere in the world and also not being used for the public. In simple terms, anything which is new which has not been disclosed anywhere can be patented.

The second criterion is an inventive step. This is also called the non-obviousness, which is a tricky part where an understanding of the prior art comes into the picture. One prior art document or several prior art documents read together with an understanding of the person skilled in the art is the key to understanding the inventive step. Even knowledge in the common domain is used for checking the inventive step.

Similar inventions or inventions having any relevant feature which club with another invention with the mind of the person skilled in the art, can obviously combine the invention or more inventions into one and come up with the existing invention, then that will be called an obvious invention.

The process is called mosaic of prior arts leading to the invention.

## What is not Anticipation

An invention claimed in a complete specification shall not be deemed to have been anticipated by reason only that the invention was published before the priority date of the relevant claim of the specification, if the patentee or the applicant for the patent proves that the matter published was obtained from him, or (where he is not himself the true and first inventor) from any person from whom he derives title, and was published without his consent or the consent of any such person; and where the patentee or the applicant for the patent or any person from whom he derives title learned of the publication before the date of the application for the patent, or, in the case of a convention application, before the date of the application for protection in a convention country, that the application or the application in the convention country, as the case may be, was made as soon as reasonably practicable thereafter.

Where a complete specification is filed in pursuance of an application for a patent made by a person being the true and first inventor or deriving title from him, an invention claimed in that specification shall not be deemed to have been anticipated by reason only of any other application for a patent in respect of the same invention made in contravention of the rights of that person, or by reason only that after the date of filing of that other application the invention was used or published, without the consent of that person, by the applicant in respect of that other application, or by any other person in consequence of any disclosure of any invention by that applicant.

An invention claimed in a complete specification shall not be deemed to have been anticipated by reason only of the communication of the invention to the Government or to any person authorized by the Government to investigate the invention or its merits, or of anything done, in consequence of such a communication, for the purpose of the investigation.

An invention claimed in a complete specification shall not be deemed to have been anticipated by reason only of the display of the invention with the consent of the true and first inventor or a person deriving title from him at an industrial or other exhibition to which the provisions of this section have been extended by the Central Government by notification in the Official Gazette, or the use thereof with his consent for the purpose of such an exhibition in the place where it is held; or the publication of any description of the invention in consequence of the display or use of the invention at any such exhibition as aforesaid; or the use of the invention, after it has been displayed or used at any such exhibition as aforesaid and during the period of the exhibition, by any person without the consent of the true and first inventor or a person deriving title from him; or

The description of the invention in a paper read by the true and first inventor before a learned society or published with his consent in the transactions of such a society.

If the application for the patent is made by the true and first inventor or a person deriving title from him not later than twelve months after the opening of the exhibition or the reading or publication of the paper, as the case may be.

An invention claimed in a complete specification shall not be deemed to have been anticipated by reason only that at any time within one year before the priority date of the relevant claim of the specification, the invention was publicly worked in India by the patentee or applicant for the patent or any person from whom he derives title; or by any other person with the consent of the patentee or applicant for the patent or any person from whom he derives title.

if the working was effected for the purpose of reasonable trial only and if it was reasonably necessary, having regard to the nature of the invention, that the working for that purpose should be effected in public.

## Patent Process

Flow chart of the Patent process in India:

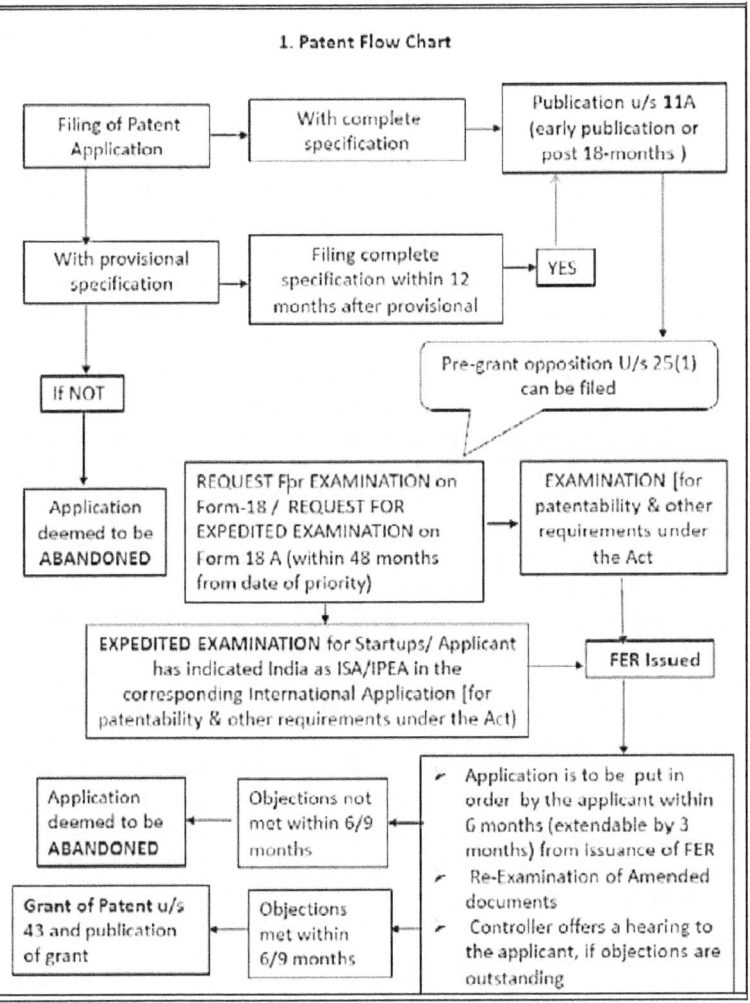

# Chapter 3 - Patent Analytics for Business

## Prior Art Search

Prior art is the information that is available prior to the effective date of a patent application, the effective date is typically the filing date of the patent application. Prior Art includes any public document, for example, published patents, technical publications such as journal articles, conference papers, websites, available products, marketing information, and the like.

## Importance of Searches

A prior art search relates to an organized review of prior art material available from public sources, and may be provided in the form of Patentability searches, Patent examination searches, Validity searches, State-of-the-art searches, Prior Art searches may also be used to determine the value of a potential investment.

A patentability search prior to filing a patent may speed up prosecution of a patent, as the claims may be configured to take into account the prior art. This may reduce overall costs by saving time, as potential future hurdles may be avoided.

A patent examination search during the prosecution of a patent is done by an examiner to determine if the patent application may be granted, which allows the examiner to comment on the novelty and inventiveness of the patent application.

A patent validity search after the grant of a patent may be done by a party who wants to contest the validity of a patent, or by a party who wishes to defend their patent, which may indicate that a patent is valid, or that it was incorrectly granted and should be revoked or could be saved by amendment.

## Art of Searching

Before searching one must understand the invention before start to search. If an invention is not fully understood non-relevant results may be deemed to be relevant. The patentability of an invention is determined with reference to the claims and interpretation of the claims in light of the specification. Many iterations may be required to obtain a suitable result. Prior art searching is an art that is learned over time.

The following steps can be used for planning and conducting searches:
1. Determine the purpose of the search
2. Acquire the necessary data to conduct the search
3. Determine which databases need to be searched
4. Develop a search strategy
5. Perform a search
6. Analyze the results
7. Modify the search strategy
8. Repeat the search
9. Analyze and summarize the results

10. Prepare report

Identification of essential features and keywords is very much required to conduct proper searches. Classification of the invention based on international classification and the category of the invention will help in generating a better result.

When a relevant prior art document has been identified, look at the prior art documents that were cited against it during its prosecution, and at patent applications against which it was cited. This may provide a significant number of prior art documents that may be equally or more relevant

Remember that an entire patent specification is important for patentability searches, not only the claims, everything that is published is prior art.

Patents and/or patent applications may be published later, but with an earlier priority date, and maybe prior art although not yet available can be relevant.

## Where to Search

There are free and paid databases to conduct a prior art search.

National or international databases are free as patents and patent applications are public information. Google Patent is one of the good resources. Espacenet and Patentscope of WIPO are also equally good free databases with lots of patent information available.

Data sources should include patent and non-patent literature. Results are used to draft claims that avoid the prior art and to focus the application on the novel and non-obvious features of the invention.

## Freedom to Operate

Freedom to operate searches are very important for businesses to check that the product has no feature, which can infringe upon the patent of any person, and if so, from whom to take licenses to operate freely in the market without any fear of infringement suit.

Patent data sources include non-expired patents that potentially related to product or service in the countries of interest only. The main idea is to determine whether an enforceable patent claims the same subject matter as features of the product or services.

## Invalidation Search

Search to find invalidating references for a patent of interest is one of the important searches especially in case of an infringement suit.

## Landscape Search

To identify business opportunities for products and services and help the Research and Development wing to focus on a subject matter of importance, patent literature and non-patent literature databases are searched and areas of improvement are identified.

Information for the search is derived from business

development and scientific leadership, where results are used to support the development of business plans and are not intended for an opinion on patentability.

# Chapter 4 - Patent Specification

Every specification, whether provisional or complete, shall describe the invention and shall begin with a title sufficiently indicating the subject-matter to which the invention relates.

Every complete specification shall have a background, summary, description, drawings, claims, and abstract.

If the applicant mentions a biological material in the specification which may not be described completely in the description, and if such material is not available to the public, the application shall be completed by depositing the material to an international depositary authority under the Budapest Treaty.

## Description

fully and particularly describe the invention and its operation or use and the method by which it is to be performed. The description must disclose the best method of performing the invention which is known to the applicant and for which he is entitled to claim protection.

The claims must be enabled by the description and nothing which is claimed should be left out of the description.

## Drawings

Drawings must be in the proper sketch format and not to be a picture of a product or process.

## Claims

A claim or claims defining the scope of the invention for which protection is claimed. The claim or claims of a complete specification shall relate to a single invention, or to a group of inventions linked so as to form a single inventive concept, shall be clear and succinct, and shall be fairly based on the matter disclosed in the specification.

A complete specification filed after a provisional specification may include claims in respect of developments of, or additions to, the invention which was described in the provisional specification, being developments or additions.

A claim is the soul of the Patent application, as the rights are solely determined by the matter defined by the claim.

## Abstract

An abstract must provide technical information on the invention.

There are several resources available for patent specification drafting which itself is a subject matter of different books. The brief information is provided here for understanding the requirement.

# Chapter 5 - Patent Procedures

## Filing

The Patent application is filed along with the Application form and specification. Statement of disclosure of foreign application and declaration of inventorship are two important forms to be filed along with the application.

Fee can be paid by demand draft or cheque for offline filing. For online filing, a reduction in fee of 10 percent is provided for the encouragement of online filing.

Where a fee is payable in respect of the filing of a document at the patent office, the fee shall be paid along with the document and the document shall be deemed not to have been filed at the office if the fee has not been paid within such time.

## Publication

No application for patent shall ordinarily be open to the public for 18 months from the date of filing of the application.

An applicant may file an application for the early publication of the application.

Every application for a patent shall, on the expiry of 18 month period be published, except in cases where the application in which secrecy direction is imposed or has been abandoned or has been withdrawn three months prior to the publication period of 18 month.

The publication of every application under this section shall include the particulars of the date of application, number of application, name, and address of the applicant identifying the application and an abstract.

Upon publication of an application for a patent, the documents are available on the patent office website for the public.

On and from the date of publication of the application for patent and until the date of grant of a patent in respect of such application, the applicant shall have the like privileges and rights as if a patent for the invention had been granted on the date of publication of the application.

## Secrecy Direction

Where it appears to the Controller that the invention is one of a class notified to him by the Central Government as relevant for defense purposes, or, where otherwise the invention appears to him to be so relevant, he may give directions for prohibiting or restricting the publication of information with respect to the invention or the communication of such information.

## Foreign Filing License

No person resident in India shall without the authority of a written permit granted by or on behalf of the Controller, make or cause to be made any application outside India for the grant of a patent for an invention unless an application for a patent for the same invention has been made in India, not less than six weeks before the application outside India.

## Amendments

No amendment of an application for a patent or a complete specification or any document relating thereto shall be made except by way of disclaimer, correction, or explanation, and no amendment thereof shall be allowed, except for the purpose of incorporation of actual fact, and no amendment of a complete specification shall be allowed, the effect of which would be that the specification as amended would claim or describe matter, not in substance disclosed or shown in the specification before the amendment, or that any claim of the specification as amended would not fall wholly within the scope of a claim of the specification before the amendment.

The Controller may, upon application made by an applicant for a patent or by a patentee, allow the application for the patent or the complete specification or any document relating thereto to be amended subject to such conditions, if any, as the Controller thinks fit.

Every application for leave to amend an application for a patent or a complete specification or any document relating thereto shall state the nature of the proposed amendment, and shall give full particulars of the reasons for which the application is made.

Any application for leave to amend an application for a patent or a complete specification or a document related thereto made after the grant of patent and the nature of the proposed amendment may be published.

The most important criterion of an amendment to specification is that no new subject matter is added in the claims and all amendments to the specification must have a basis in the originally filed specification.

## Examination

No application for a patent shall be examined unless the applicant or any other interested person makes a request for such examination within the prescribed period.

In case the applicant or any other interested person does not make a request for examination of the application for a patent within 48 months from the date of application, the application shall be treated as withdrawn by the applicant.

The Patent Examiner shall check the following:

(a) whether the application and the specification and other documents relating thereto are in accordance with the requirements of the Patent Act and of any rules made thereunder;

(b) whether there is any lawful ground of objection to the grant of the patent under the Patent Act in pursuance of the application;

(c) the result of investigations made by prior art search; and

(d) any other matter related to provisions of patent law.

The examiner to whom the application and the specification and other documents relating thereto are referred shall ordinarily make the report to the Controller.

The examiner to whom an application for a patent is referred shall make an investigation for the purpose of ascertaining whether the invention so far as claimed in any claim of the complete specification has been anticipated by publication before the date of filing of the applicant's complete specification in any specification filed in pursuance of an application for a patent made in India or anticipated by claimed in any claim of any other complete specification published on or after the date of filing of the applicant's complete specification, being a specification filed in pursuance of an application for a patent made in India and dated before or claiming the priority date earlier than that date.

The examiner shall, in addition, make such investigation for the purpose of ascertaining whether the invention, so far as claimed in any claim of the complete specification, has been anticipated by publication in India or elsewhere in any document.

The examination and investigations shall not be deemed in any way to warrant the validity of any patent, and no liability shall be incurred by the Central Government or any officer thereof by reason of, or in connection with, any such examination or investigation or any report or other proceedings consequent thereon.

Where it appears to the Controller that the invention so far as claimed in any claim of the complete specification has been anticipated in the manner he may refuse the application unless the applicant shows to the satisfaction of the Controller that the priority date of the claim of his complete specification is not later than the date on which the relevant document was published, or amends his complete specification to the satisfaction of the Controller.

If it appears to the Controller that the invention is claimed in a claim of any other complete specification he may, direct that a reference to that other specification shall be inserted by way of notice to the public in the applicant's complete specification unless within such time as may be prescribed, the applicant shows to the satisfaction of the Controller that the priority date of his claim is not later than the priority date of the claim of the said another specification; or the complete specification is amended to the satisfaction of the Controller.

## Grant

Where the Controller is satisfied that the application or any specification or any other document filed in pursuance thereof does not comply with the requirements of the Patent Act or of any rules made thereunder, the Controller may refuse the application or may require the application, specification, or the other documents, as the case may be, to be amended to his satisfaction before he proceeds with the application and refuses the application on failure to do so.

An application for a patent shall be deemed to have been abandoned unless, within 6 months (extendable to 9 months), the applicant has complied with all the requirements imposed on him, whether in connection with the complete specification or otherwise in relation to the application.

Once the Patent application is in order and all criteria of patentability are met, the Controller shall grant the patent.

On the grant of a patent, the Controller shall publish the fact that the patent has been granted and thereupon the application, specification and other documents related thereto shall be open for public inspection.

The date of every patent shall be entered in the register.

No suit or other proceeding shall be commenced or prosecuted in respect of an infringement committed before the date of publication of the application.
Every patent shall be in the prescribed form and shall have effect throughout India.

A patent shall be granted for one invention only.

## Appeal

A person aggrieved by the decision of the Controller may file an appeal to the Intellectual Property Appellate Board (IPAB).

IPAB is a quasi-judicial body and deals with the appeal matters against the decision of the Controller. The revocation proceeding for a patent can be initiated in IPAB.

## Renewal

A renewal fee is required to be paid for continuing the patent protection from the third year of the filing of the patent, which is payable only after the grant of a patent.

If the renewal fee is not paid the patent shall cease to exist. Where a patent has ceased to have an effect by reason of failure to pay any renewal fee, the patentee with the leave of the Controller, may within eighteen months from the date on which the patent ceased to have an effect, make an application for the restoration of the patent.

An application for restoration shall contain a statement, verified in the prescribed manner, fully setting out the circumstances which led to the failure to pay the prescribed fee, and the Controller may require from the applicant such further evidence as he may think necessary.

If, after hearing the applicant in cases where the applicant so desires or the Controller thinks fit, the Controller is prima facie satisfied that the failure to pay the renewal fee was unintentional and that there has been no undue delay in the making of the application, he shall publish the application.

The failure to pay the renewal fee should not be intentional, or there has not been undue delay in the making of the application.

Where a patent is restored, the rights of the patentee shall be subject to such provisions as may be prescribed and to such other provisions as the Controller thinks fit to impose for the protection or compensation of persons who may have begun to avail themselves of, or have taken definite steps by contract or otherwise to avail themselves of, the patented invention between the date when the patent ceased to have an effect and the date of publication of the application for restoration of the patent.

No suit or other proceeding shall be commenced or prosecuted in respect of an infringement of a patent committed between the date on which the patent ceased to have an effect and the date of the publication of the application for restoration of the patent.

Where a principal patent is granted later than two years from the date of the filing of the application, the fees which have become due in the meantime may be paid within a term of three months from the date of the recording of the patent in the register or within the extended period not later than nine months from the date of recording.

# Chapter 6 - Type of Patent Application

## Ordinary Application

Where an application, for a patent is accompanied by a provisional specification, a complete specification shall be filed within twelve months from the date of filing of the application, and if the complete specification is not so filed, the application shall be deemed to be abandoned.

Where two or more applications in the name of the same applicant are accompanied by provisional specifications in respect of inventions which are cognate or of which one is a modification of another and the Controller is of opinion that the whole of such inventions are such as to constitute a single invention and may properly be included in one patent, he may allow one complete specification to be filed in respect of all such provisional specifications.

Where an application for a patent is accompanied by a specification purporting to be a complete specification, the Controller may, if the applicant so requests at any time within twelve months from the date of filing of the application, direct that such specification shall be treated as a provisional specification and proceed with the application accordingly.

Where a complete specification has been filed in pursuance of an application for a patent accompanied by a provisional specification the Controller may, if the applicant so requests at any time before granting of a patent, cancel the provisional specification and post-date the application to the date of filing of the complete specification.

## Convention Application

Convention country means a country or a country that is a member of a group of countries or a union of countries or an Inter-governmental organization being a member of the Paris Convention or any bilateral treaty with India for patent protection.

Any country, which is a signatory or party or a group of countries, union of countries or intergovernmental organizations which are signatories or parties to an international, regional or bi-lateral treaty, convention or arrangement to which India is also a signatory or party and which affords to the applicants for patents in India or to citizens of India similar privileges as are granted to their own citizens or citizens to their member countries in respect of the grant of patents and protection of patent rights shall be a convention country or convention countries.

Where a person has made an application for a patent in respect of an invention in a Convention country and that person or the legal representative or assignee of that person makes an application for a patent within twelve months after the date on which the basic application was made, the priority date of a claim of the complete specification, being a claim based on the matter disclosed in the basic application, is the date of making of the basic application.

Where applications have been made for similar protection in respect of an invention in two or more convention countries, the period of twelve months shall be reckoned from the date on which the earlier or earliest of the said applications were made.

Every convention application shall be accompanied by a complete specification; and specify the date on which and the convention country in which the application for protection, or as the case may be, the first of such applications were made; and state that no application for protection in respect of the invention had been made in a convention country before that date by the applicant or by any person from whom he derives title.

The priority date of the convention application shall be the date of basic application in a convention country.

If any specification or other document is in a foreign language, a translation into English of the specification or document, verified by affidavit or otherwise to the satisfaction of the Controller, shall be furnished when required by the Controller.

All the provisions of the patent procedure shall apply in relation to a convention application and a patent granted in pursuance thereof as they apply in relation to an ordinary application and a patent granted in pursuance thereof.

## PCT application

International application through PCT application provides several benefits, as explained in chapter 11.

An international application filed under the Patent Cooperation Treaty designating India shall have the title, description, claim, and abstract, and drawings, if any, filed in the international application shall be taken as complete specification.

The filing date of application for patent and its complete specification processed by the patent office as designated office shall be the international filing date accorded under the Patent Cooperation Treaty.

Amendment, if any, proposed by the applicant for an international application designating India or designating and electing India before an international searching authority or preliminary examination authority shall, if the applicant so desires, be taken as an amendment made before the patent office.

**Divisional application**

A person who has made an application for a patent, at any time before the grant of the patent, if he so desires, or with a view to remedying the objection raised by the Controller on the ground that the claims of the complete specification relating to more than one invention, file a further application in respect of an invention disclosed in the provisional or complete specification already filed in respect of the first-mentioned application.

The divisional application shall be accompanied by a complete specification, but such complete specification shall not include any matter, not in substance disclosed in the complete specification filed in pursuance of the first-mentioned application.

The Controller may require such amendment of the complete specification filed in pursuance of either the original or the further application as may be necessary to ensure that neither of the said complete specifications includes a claim for any matter claimed in the other.

The Divisional application and the complete specification accompanying it shall be deemed to have been filed on the date on which the first-mentioned application had been filed, and the further application shall be proceeded with as a substantive application and be examined when the request for examination is filed within the prescribed period.

## Patent of Addition

Where an application is made for a patent in respect of any improvement in or modification of an invention described or disclosed in the complete specification filed therefor and the applicant also applies or has applied for a patent for that invention in respect thereof, the Controller may, if the applicant so requests grant the patent for the improvement or modification as a patent of addition.

Where an invention, being an improvement in or modification of another invention, is the subject of an independent patent and the patentee in respect of that patent is also the patentee in respect of the patent for the main invention, the Controller may, if the patentee so requests, by order, revoke the patent for the improvement or modification and grant to the patentee a patent of addition in respect thereof, bearing the same date as the date of the patent so revoked.

A patent shall not be granted as a patent of addition unless the date of filing of the application was the same as or later than the date of filing of the application in respect of the main invention.

A patent of addition shall not be granted before the grant of the patent for the main invention. A patent of addition shall be granted for a term equal to that of the patent for the main invention shall remain in force during that term of the patent for the main invention and no longer.

No renewal fees shall be payable in respect of a patent of addition, but, if any such patent becomes an independent patent the same fees shall thereafter be payable, upon the same dates, as if the patent had been originally granted as an independent patent.

The grant of a patent of addition shall not be refused, and a patent granted as a patent of addition shall not be revoked or invalidated, on the ground only that the invention claimed in the complete specification does not involve any inventive step having regard to any publication or use of the main invention described in the complete specification relating thereto and the validity of a patent of addition shall not be questioned on the ground that the invention ought to have been the subject of an independent patent. The novelty of the invention claimed in the patent of addition shall be a requirement.

# Chapter 7 - Opposition

## Type of Opposition
Where an application has been published, any person can file an opposition to the grant of patent. Such opposition is called as pre-grant opposition.

Where a patent has been granted, any person interested can file an opposition against the grant of a patent within a year. Such opposition is called as post-grant opposition.

## Grounds of Opposition
The Grounds for pre-grant opposition under Section 25(1) of the Patents Act, are:

(a) that the applicant for the patent or the person under or through whom he claims, wrongfully obtained the invention or any part thereof from him or from a person under or through whom he claims;

(b) that the invention so far as claimed in any claim of the complete specification has been published before the priority date of the claim in any specification filed in India or elsewhere or in any other document;

(c) that the invention so far as claimed in any claim of the complete specification is claimed in a claim of a complete specification published on or after the priority date of the applicant's claim and filed in pursuance of an application for a patent in India, being a claim of which the priority date is earlier than that of the applicant's claim;

(d) that the invention so far as claimed in any claim of the complete specification was publicly known or publicly used in India before the priority date of that claim.

(e) that the invention so far as claimed in any claim of the complete specification is obvious and clearly does not involve any inventive step, having regard to the matter published or having regard to what was used in India before the priority date of the applicant's claim;

(f) that the subject of any claim of the complete specification is not an invention within the meaning of the Patents Act or is not patentable under the Patents Act;

(g) that the complete specification does not sufficiently and clearly describe the invention or the method by which it is to be performed;

(h) that the applicant has failed to disclose to the Controller the information regarding foreign applications or has furnished the information which in any material particular was false to his knowledge;

(i) that in the case of a convention application, the application was not made within twelve months from the date of the first application for protection for the invention made in a convention country by the applicant or a person from whom he derives title;

(j) that the complete specification does not disclose or wrongly mentions the source or geographical origin of biological material used for the invention;

(k) that the invention so far as claimed in any claim of the complete specification is anticipated having regard to the knowledge, oral or otherwise, available within any local or indigenous community in India or elsewhere,

The Grounds of post-grant opposition under Section 25(2) of the Patents Act are:

(a) that the patentee or the person under or through whom he claims, wrongfully obtained the invention or any part thereof from him or from a person under or through whom he claims;

(b) that the invention so far as claimed in any claim of the complete specification has been published before the priority date of the claim in any specification filed in India or elsewhere, or in any other document;

(c) that the invention so far as claimed in any claim of the complete specification is claimed in a claim of a complete specification published on or after the priority date of the claim of the patentee and filed in pursuance of an application for a patent in India, being a claim of which the priority date is earlier than that of the claim of the patentee;

(d) that the invention so far as claimed in any claim of the complete specification was publicly known or publicly used in India before the priority date of that claim;

(e) that the invention so far as claimed in any claim of the complete specification is obvious and clearly does not involve any inventive step, having regard to the matter published or having regard to what was used in India before the priority date of the claim;

(f) that the subject of any claim of the complete specification is not an invention within the meaning of the Patents Act or is not patentable under the Patents Act;

(g) that the complete specification does not sufficiently and clearly describe the invention or the method by which it is to be performed;

(h) that the patentee has failed to disclose to the Controller the information required by section 8 or has furnished the information which in any material particular was false to his knowledge;

(i) that in the case of a patent granted on a convention application, the application for a patent was not made within twelve months from the date of the first application for protection for the invention made in a convention country or in India by the patentee or a person from whom he derives title;

(j) that the complete specification does not disclose or wrongly mentions the source and geographical origin of biological material used for the invention; and

(k) that the invention so far as claimed in any claim of the complete specification was anticipated having regard to the knowledge, oral or otherwise, available within any local or indigenous community in India or elsewhere.

## Who can File an Opposition

Any person can file the pre-grant opposition.

A person interested can file the post-grant opposition. Person interested includes a person engaged in, or in promoting, research in the same field as that to which the invention relates.

## Procedure of Opposition

When the notice of opposition filed by the opponent, the Controller shall notify the patentee.

On receipt of notice of opposition by the Controller shall constitute a Board to be known as the Opposition Board consisting of such officers as he may determine and refer such notice of opposition along with the documents to that Board for examination and submission of its recommendations to the Controller.

Every Opposition Board shall conduct the examination.

On receipt of the recommendation of the Opposition Board and after giving the patentee and the opponent an opportunity of being heard, the Controller shall order either to maintain or to amend or to revoke the patent.

The Controller in the opposition proceedings shall have the following power of the civil court
    (a) summoning and enforcing the attendance of any person and examining him on oath;

    (b) requiring the discovery and production of any document;

    (c) receiving evidence on affidavits;

    (d) issuing commissions for the examination of witnesses or documents;

    (e) awarding costs;

    (f) reviewing his own decision on an application made within the prescribed time and in a prescribed manner; and

    (g) setting aside an order passed ex- parte on

an application made within the prescribed time and in the prescribed manner.

In the opposition proceedings opportunity to provide evidence and expert opinion is allowed in favor and against the patentability criteria of the application.

# Chapter 8 - Patent Infringement

Patent infringement is defined as the infringement of patent rights by any unauthorized use of a patented product or process by a third party.

Patented article and patented process means respectively an article or process in respect of which a patent is in force.

On and from the date of publication of the application for patent and until the date of grant of a patent in respect of such application, the applicant shall have the like privileges and rights as if a patent for the invention had been granted on the date of publication of the application.

The applicant shall not be entitled to institute any proceedings for infringement until the patent has been granted.

## Filing Suits in Courts

The jurisdiction of the civil court has to be ascertained under the Code of Civil Procedure, 1908.

No suit for infringement of a patent shall be instituted in any court inferior to a district court having jurisdiction to try the suit, which is determined under the rules made by different High Courts.

The aggrieved party, in case of patent infringement, the patentee, or a licensee may institute the suit. The assignment or license must be registered with the Patent Office to have a right to file an infringement suit.

In any suit for infringement of a patent, where the subject matter of the patent is a process for obtaining a product, the court may direct the defendant to prove that the process used by him to obtain the product, identical to the product of the patented process, is different from the patented process if,—

(a) the subject matter of the patent is a process for obtaining a new product; or

(b) there is a substantial likelihood that the identical product is made by the process, and the patentee or a person deriving title or interest in the patent from him, has been unable through reasonable efforts to determine the process actually used.

Provided that the patentee or a person deriving title or interest in the patent from him first proves that the product is identical to the product directly obtained by the patented process.

The holder of an exclusive license shall have the like right as the patentee to institute a suit in respect of any infringement of the patent committed after the date of the license, and in awarding damages or an account of profits or granting any other relief in any such suit the court shall take into consideration any loss suffered or likely to be suffered by the exclusive licensee as such or, as the case may be, the profits earned by means of the infringement so far as it constitutes an infringement of the rights of the exclusive licensee as such.

In any suit for infringement of a patent by the holder of an exclusive license the patentee shall, unless he has joined as a plaintiff in the suit, be added as a defendant, but a patentee so added as defendant shall not be liable for any costs unless he enters an appearance and takes part in the proceedings.

## Defenses to Infringements

In any suit for infringement of a patent every ground on which it may be revoked shall be available as a ground for defense.

In any suit for infringement of a patent by the making, using or importation of any machine, apparatus or other article or by the user of any process or by the importation, use or distribution or any medicine or drug, it shall be a ground for a defense that such making, using, importation or distribution is in accordance with fair use.

The person or persons registered as grantee or proprietor of a patent shall have the power to assign, grant licenses under, or otherwise deal with, the patent and to give effectual receipts for any consideration for any such assignment, license, or dealing. Provided that any equities in respect of the patent may be enforced in like manner as in respect of any other movable property.

In a suit for infringement of patent, damages or an account of profits shall not be granted against the defendant who proves that at the date of the infringement he was not aware and had no reasonable grounds for believing that the patent existed.

A person shall not be deemed to have been aware or to have had reasonable grounds for believing that a patent exists by reason only of the application to an article of the word "patent", "patented" or any word or words expressing or implying that a patent has been obtained for the article unless the number of the patent accompanies the word or words in question.

In any suit for infringement of a patent the court may, if it thinks fit, refuse to grant any damages or an account of profits in respect of any infringement committed after a failure to pay any renewal fee within the prescribed period and before any extension of that period.

Where an amendment of a specification by way of disclaimer, correction, or explanation has been allowed under this Act after the publication of the specification, no damages or account of profits shall be granted in any proceeding in respect of the use of the invention before the date of the decision allowing the amendment, unless the court is satisfied that the specification as originally published was framed in good faith and with reasonable skill and knowledge.

The court has the power to grant an injunction in any suit for infringement of a patent and that has been used in India. Almost in 80-90% of cases, an interim injunction has been granted for infringement suits in India.

## Fair Use

The following shall be taken as fair use:

(a) any act of making, constructing, using, selling or importing a patented invention solely for uses reasonably related to the development and submission of information required under any law for the time being in force, in India, or in a country other than India, that regulates the manufacture, construction, use, sale or import of any product; and

(b) importation of patented products by any person from a person who is duly authorized under the law to produce and sell or distribute the product, shall not be considered as an infringement of patent rights.

The passing vehicle having a patent product stopped at any port on Indian jurisdiction, which is bound for another country shall not be taken as infringement, which is called a Bolar exemption.

## Revocation

The Patent can be revoked by filing a petition to the IPAB or in the matter of infringement suit under any of the following grounds:

(a) that the invention, so far as claimed in any claim of the complete specification, was claimed in a valid claim of earlier priority date contained in the complete specification of another patent granted in India;

(b) that the patent was granted on the application of a person not entitled under the provisions of the Patent Act to apply therefor:

(c) that the patent was obtained wrongfully in contravention of the rights of the petitioner or any person under or through whom he claims;

(d) that the subject of any claim of the complete specification is not an invention within the meaning of the Patent Act;

(e) that the invention so far as claimed in any claim of the complete specification is not new, having regard to what was publicly known or publicly used in India before the priority date of the claim or to what was published in India or elsewhere in any of the documents;

(f) that the invention so far as claimed in any claim of the complete specification is obvious or does not involve any inventive step, having regard to what was publicly known or publicly used in India or what was published in India or elsewhere before the priority date of the claim;

(g) that the invention, so far as claimed in any claim of the complete specification, is not useful;

(h) that the complete specification does not sufficiently and fairly describe the invention and the method by which it is to be performed, that is to say, that the description of the method or the instructions for the working of the invention as contained in the complete specification are not by themselves sufficient to enable a person in India possessing average skill in, and average knowledge of, the art to which the invention relates, to work the invention, or that it does not disclose the best method of performing it which was known to the applicant for the patent and for which he was entitled to claim protection;

(i) that the scope of any claim of the complete specification is not sufficiently and clearly defined or that any claim of the complete specification is not fairly based on the matter disclosed in the specification;

(j) that the patent was obtained on a false suggestion or representation;

(k) that the subject of any claim of the complete specification is not patentable under the Patents Act;

(l) that the invention so far as claimed in any claim of the complete specification was secretly used in India, before the priority date of the claim;

(m) that the applicant for the patent has failed to disclose to the Controller the information required about foreign application or has furnished information which in any material particular was false to his knowledge;

(n) that the applicant contravened any direction for secrecy or made or caused to be made an application for the grant of a patent outside India in contravention of the Patents Act;

(o) that leave to amend the complete specification was obtained by fraud.

(p) that the complete specification does not disclose or wrongly mentions the source or geographical origin of biological material used for the invention; and

(q) that the invention so far as claimed in any claim of the complete specification was anticipated having regard to the knowledge, oral or otherwise, available within any local or indigenous community in India or elsewhere.

Notice of any petition for revocation of a patent shall be served on all persons appearing from the register to be proprietors of that patent or to have shares or interests therein and it shall not be necessary to serve a notice on any other person.

## Injunction

The reliefs which a court may grant in any suit for infringement include an injunction and, at the option of the plaintiff, either damages or an account of profits.

The court may also order that the goods which are found to be infringing and materials and implements, the predominant use of which is in the creation of infringing goods shall be seized, forfeited, or destroyed, as the court deems fit under the circumstances of the case without payment of any compensation.

If in proceedings for infringement of a patent it is found that any claim of the specification, being a claim in respect of which infringement is alleged, is valid, but that any other claim is invalid, the court may grant relief in respect of any valid claim which is infringed.

Where the plaintiff proves that the invalid claim was framed in good faith and with reasonable skill and knowledge, the court shall grant relief in respect of any valid claim which is infringed subject to the discretion of the court as to costs and as to the date from which damages or an account of profits should be reckoned, and in exercising such discretion the court may take into consideration the conduct of the parties in inserting such invalid claims in the specification or permitting them to remain there.

## Groundless Threats

Where any person (whether entitled to or interested in a patent or an application for patent or not) threatens any other person by circulars or advertisements or by communications, oral or in writing addressed to that or any other person, with proceedings for infringement of a patent, any person aggrieved thereby may bring a suit against him praying for the following reliefs, that is to say—

(a) a declaration to the effect that the threats are unjustifiable;

(b) an injunction against the continuance of the threats; and

(c) such damages, if any, as he has sustained thereby.

Unless in such suit the defendant proves that the acts in respect of which the proceedings were threatened constitute or, if done, would constitute, an infringement of a patent or of rights arising from the publication of a complete specification in respect of a claim of the specification not shown by the plaintiff to be invalid the court may grant to the plaintiff all or any of the reliefs prayed for.

Mere notification of the existence of a patent does not constitute a threat of proceeding within the meaning of this section.

## Settlements

A Patent infringement suit being a civil matter can be settled outside court. A strong patent portfolio always helps in settling disputes amicably.

# Chapter 9 - Rights of Patentee

## Right to Exploit Patent
Where the subject matter of the patent is a product, the patentee has exclusive right to prevent third parties, who do not have his consent, from the act of making, using, offering for sale, selling, or importing for those purposes that product in India.

Where the subject matter of the patent is a process, the patentee has exclusive right to prevent third parties, who do not have his consent, from the act of using that process, and from the act of using, offering for sale, selling, or importing for those purposes the product obtained directly by that process in India.

Where a patent is granted to two or more persons, each of those persons shall, unless an agreement to the contrary is in force, be entitled to an equal undivided share in the patent.

## Right to License
The Patentee can grant an exclusive or non-exclusive license for a lump-sum payment or royalty, on the patent.

## Right to Assign

A Patentee can assign the rights in the patent to any person for consideration.

An assignment of a patent or of a share in a patent, a mortgage, license, or the creation of any other interest in a patent shall not be valid unless the same were in writing and the agreement between the parties concerned is reduced to the form of a document embodying all the terms and conditions governing their rights and obligations and duly executed.

Where any person becomes entitled by assignment, transmission, or operation of law to a patent or to a share in a patent or becomes entitled as a mortgagee, licensee or otherwise to any other interest in a patent, he shall apply in writing in the prescribed manner to the Controller for the registration of his title or, as the case may be, of notice of his interest in the register.

## Right to Mortgage

The Patentee can mortgage the patent, as the patent is an asset. Companies get a valuation on a patent portfolio on which they can take loans from financial institutions.

## Right to Lease

The Patentee can lease the patent rights, like any other property.

## Right to Surrender

A patentee may, at any time by giving notice in the prescribed manner to the Controller, offer to surrender his patent.

## Right against Infringement

The Patentee can sue any person infringing upon any of the patent rights, similar to rights in any other property.

## Enforcement of Patent

The Patentee has the right to enforce his patent by instituting a suit, through police and customs authorities, who may seize the products alleged to be infringing.

# Chapter 10 - Commercialization of Patent

## Use
The patents are granted to encourage inventions and to secure that the inventions are worked in India on a commercial scale and to the fullest extent that is reasonably practicable without undue delay.

The Patentee has to provide a working statement of a patent on a yearly basis to the Patent Office.

The protection and enforcement of patent rights contribute to the promotion of technological innovation and to the transfer and dissemination of technology, to the mutual advantage of producers and users of technological knowledge and in a manner conducive to social and economic welfare, and to a balance of rights and obligations.

The Patentee has the right to use, sell, or market the patented article.

## License
The Patentee can give an exclusive or non-exclusive license in the patent to any person.

An exclusive license means a license from a patentee which confers on the licensee, or on the licensee and persons authorized by him, to the exclusion of all other persons (including the patentee), any right in respect of the patented invention.

The licensee must register the license agreement with the patent office for having a right to be a party in any infringement suit.

## Technology Transfer

Patent and technology can be transferred to any person for commercial utilization.

In the case of technology transfer, the patentee must be aware that the transfer is of whole technology and not only of the patent. Such clauses having the effect of the same shall be included in the technology transfer agreement.

Technology transfer can be done for any technology even if it is not subject to any patent application or granted patent.

## Compulsory Licensing

At any time after the expiration of three years from the date of the grant of a patent, any person interested may make an application to the Controller for grant of a compulsory license on patent on any of the following grounds, namely:—

(a) that the reasonable requirements of the public with respect to the patented invention have not been satisfied,

(b) that the patented invention is not available to the public at a reasonably affordable price, or

(c) that the patented invention does not work in the territory of India.

An application for a compulsory license may be made by any person and no person shall be estopped from alleging that the reasonable requirements of the public with respect to the patented invention are not satisfied or that the patented invention is not worked in the territory of India or that the patented invention is not available to the public at a reasonably affordable price by reason of any admission made by him, whether in such a license or otherwise or by reason of his having accepted such a license.

First of a kind compulsory license has been granted in the case of Bayer vs. Natco for a cancer drug to Natco Pharma.

# Chapter 11 - PCT Application

International application means an application for a patent made in accordance with the Patent Cooperation Treaty.

Globalization is new age phenomena and inventions are worked throughout the globe, which brings the need for patent protection in other countries. Filing in every country within 12 months of the priority date as a convention application is not feasible every time.

PCT has come up with an international application, which provides the applicant a longer timeline for filing a national phase application in the country of interest.

Though the protection is always through a grant of patent in a specific country, the international search and examination provide the applicant a fair idea about the strength of the patent application and meanwhile to choose which country can be valuable for commercialization.

## PCT International Application

International applications can be filed with the International Bureau of WIPO, Geneva, and also with the Indian Patent Office depending on the place of residence of the applicant in India competent receiving offices for PCT application by Indian residents.

In case of an international application designating India, the title, description, drawings, abstract and claims filed with the application shall be taken as the complete specification for the purposes of this Act.

The application can be filed in English or French.

## International Publication
The international application shall be published after 18 months from the date of priority. The published documents can be accessed on the WIPO website.

## International Search
The International search is conducted by the chosen International Search authority, based upon the search report, the applicant can amend the claims and specification.

## International Preliminary Examination
The International preliminary examination is being conducted by the International Preliminary Examining Authority, as chosen by the applicant.

## National Phase Applications
Any time after filing the international application, the

applicant may file a national phase application in the country of interest. Generally, countries provide around 30/31 months to file a national phase application.

A national phase application shall be treated by the patent office as a normal application. and other processes remain the same after filing the national phase application.

# Chapter 12 - Startups and IP

**Definition of Startup**

The Government of India to promote innovation in the country has provided several benefits to the startup which is recognized under the Department of industrial policy and promotion (DIPP).

Eligibility Criteria for Startup Recognition:

The Startup should be incorporated as a private limited company or registered as a partnership firm or a limited liability partnership.

Turnover should be less than INR 100 Crores in any of the previous financial years.

An entity shall be considered as a startup up to 10 years from the date of its incorporation.

The Startup should be working towards innovation/ improvement of existing products, services, and processes and should have the potential to generate employment/ create wealth. An entity formed by splitting up or reconstruction of an existing business shall not be considered a startup.

## Benefits to Startup

The benefits include several mentorship and awareness programs including freebies from the startup community for the growth of business. To promote innovation, fees for patents and trademarks have also been reduced for recognized startups.

The fee for patents and trademarks is equivalent to a natural person and almost one-fifth of the fee from a company or organization.

There is a benefit to several startups in terms of tax and compliance exemptions too.

## Expedited Examination

Startups can file for expedited examination of patent applications filed by them, which reduces the time required for grant of patent.

There are cases where patents have been granted by the Indian Patent Office within 8 months from the date of filing to a startup.

www.ingramcontent.com/pod-product-compliance
Lightning Source LLC
Chambersburg PA
CBHW070424220526
45466CB00004B/1529